THE KINSMAN REDEEMER

By

Richard A. Carr Sr.

PREFACE

One of the difficult problems facing Christians today is explaining the concept of salvation in a manner that can be easily understood. This work is designed to aid Christians is explaining this new and foreign concept to those we meet in our society.

In the past we have been content to tell the world, that you are evil and without God providing salvation you will go to hell. While this is the literal truth, it does not explain why we are evil, and how and why we can change. If the concept of salvation is to be understood, we must offer some rational explanation that will answer the natural questions the peoples of the world will ask.

This work is not designed to be a complete and exhaustive explanation of all of the theological concepts of salvation. Rather it is designed to be a practical handbook for understanding God's plan of salvation. It is designed to lead the reader through the process of determining what salvation is, how it came about, who needs it, and how to obtain the benefits of it.

Please feel free to share the concepts included in the book with your friends and fellow church members. Any comments and suggestions are always welcome. Any mistakes should also be communicated so that they can be corrected.

I would be remiss if I failed to include thanks for those who have helped me so much as I worked on the concept. First of all to my wife who puts up with me and understands when I am struggling with the writing. My pastor, Rev. Joseph Peters who continues to bless me with both his words and his life. He is a shining example to all who know him. Brother Tom Leonard for his help in correcting my bad grammar and misspellings. Last but not least, to my Bible study group who are faithful to come every week for study and growth, and who never fail to give me encouragement and support as I attempt to grow in God's love.

TABLE OF CONTENTS

PREFACE i
TABLE OF CONTENTS iii
CHAPTER 1 1
  GOD!   God god? 1
  GOD VS. SCIENCE 1
CHAPTER 2 9
  WHY MAN   WHY SALVATION 9
    WHY MAN 9
    WHY SALVATION 11
CHAPTER 3 19
  SACRIFICE 19
    ADAM 19
    NOAH 20
    ABRAHAM 21
    MOSES 26
  THE LAW 33
CHAPTER 4 37
  THE LAW OF THE 37
  KINSMAN REDEEMER 37
CHAPTER 5 45
  THE TRUE KINSMAN REDEEMER 45
  THE OLD TESTAMENT SPEAKS 45
  CHRIST THE KINSMAN REDEEMER 48
CHAPTER 6 55
  YOUR CHOICE 55
  THE NEXT STEP 58

CHAPTER 1

GOD! God god?

Before we can begin to discuss the concept of salvation and how or why it might be accomplished, we must first establish that there is a God, and that He desires our salvation. In today's society we are being confronted with the concept that there is either no God or that God is dead. Everywhere we turn we meet people who have no need or use for a God. This is a fairly new concept, since as little as a hundred years ago the concept was not even recognized. Everyone knew there was a God, and that we needed a relationship with Him. It has only been in the past 100 years that society has begun to question both the existence and purpose of God. As secular education and secular humanism has been pushed upon society, we see more and more people question the existence of God.

As Christians, we must face this question head on and be prepared for the questions the world will ask us about God. Does he exist, if he does, why does he want a relationship with us, and how does all of this affect life and society today.

The following story is anecdotal and I have been unable to verify the truth of the story, but even if it did not really happen, it points out the basic conflict between believers and atheists.

GOD VS. SCIENCE

"Let me explain the problem science has with religion."
The atheist professor of philosophy pauses before his class and then asks one of his new students to stand.
'You're a Christian, aren't you, son?'
'Yes sir,' the student says.
'So you believe in God?'
'Absolutely'
'Is God good?'

'Sure! God's good.'
'Is God all-powerful? Can God do anything?'
'Yes'
'Are you good or evil?'
'The Bible says I'm evil.'
The professor grins knowingly. 'Aha! The Bible! He considers for a moment. 'Here's one for you. Let's say there's a sick person over here and you can cure him. You can do it. Would you help him? Would you try?'
'Yes sir, I would.'
'So you're good...!'
'I wouldn't say that.'
'But why not say that? You'd help a sick and maimed person if you could. Most of us would if we could. But God doesn't.'
The student does not answer, so the professor continues. 'He doesn't, does he? My brother was a Christian who died of cancer, even though he prayed to Jesus to heal him. How is this Jesus good? Can you answer that one?'
The student remains silent. 'No, you can't, can you?' the professor says. He takes a sip of water from a glass on his desk to give the student time to relax. 'Let's start again, young fella. Is God good?'
'Er..yes,' the student says.
'Is Satan good?'
The student doesn't hesitate on this one. 'No.'
'Then where does Satan come from?'
The student falters. 'From God'
'That's right. God made Satan, didn't he? Tell me, son. Is there evil in this world?'
'Yes, sir.'
'Evil's everywhere, isn't it? And God did make everything, correct?'
'Yes'
'So who created evil?' The professor continued, 'If God created everything, then God created evil, since evil exists, and according to the principle that our works define who we are, then God is evil.'

Again, the student has no answer. 'Is there sickness? Immorality? Hatred? Ugliness? All these terrible things, do they exist in this world?'
The student squirms on his feet. 'Yes.'
'So who created them?'
The student does not answer again, so the professor repeats his question. 'Who created them?' There is still no answer. Suddenly the lecturer breaks away to pace in front of the classroom. The class is mesmerized. 'Tell me,' he continues onto another student. 'Do you believe in Jesus Christ, son?'
The student's voice betrays him and cracks. 'Yes, professor, I do.'
The old man stops pacing. 'Science says you have five senses you use to identify and observe the world around you. Have you ever seen Jesus?'
'No sir. I've never seen Him.'
'Then tell us if you've ever heard your Jesus?'
'No, sir, I have not.'
'Have you ever felt your Jesus, tasted your Jesus or smelt your Jesus? Have you ever had any sensory perception of Jesus Christ, or God for that matter?'
'No, sir, I'm afraid I haven't.'
'Yet you still believe in him?'
'Yes'
'According to the rules of empirical, testable, demonstrable protocol, science says your God doesn't exist... What do you say to that, son?'
'Nothing,' the student replies. 'I only have my faith.'
'Yes, faith,' the professor repeats. 'And that is the problem science has with God. There is no evidence, only faith.'
The student stands quietly for a moment, before asking a question of His own. 'Professor, is there such thing as heat?'
'Yes.
'And is there such a thing as cold?'
'Yes, son, there's cold too.'
'No sir, there isn't.'
The professor turns to face the student, obviously interested. The room suddenly becomes very quiet. The

student begins to explain. 'You can have lots of heat, even more heat, super-heat, mega-heat, unlimited heat, white heat, a little heat or no heat, but we don't have anything called 'cold'. We can hit down to 458 degrees below zero, which is no heat, but we can't go any further after that. There is no such thing as cold; otherwise we would be able to go colder than the lowest -458 degrees. Everybody or object is susceptible to study when it has or transmits energy, and heat is what makes a body or matter have or transmit energy. Absolute zero (-458 F) is the total absence of heat. You see, sir, cold is only a word we use to describe the absence of heat. We cannot measure cold. Heat we can measure in thermal units because heat is energy. Cold is not the opposite of heat, sir, just the absence of it.'

Silence across the room. A pen drops somewhere in the classroom, sounding like a hammer.

'What about darkness, professor. Is there such a thing as darkness?'

'Yes,' the professor replies without hesitation. 'What is night if it isn't darkness?'

'You're wrong again, sir. Darkness is not something; it is the absence of something. You can have low light, normal light, bright light, flashing light, but if you have no light constantly you have nothing and it's called darkness, isn't it? That's the meaning we use to define the word. In reality, darkness isn't. If it were, you would be able to make darkness darker, wouldn't you?'

The professor begins to smile at the student in front of him. This will be a good semester. 'So what point are you making, young man?'

'Yes, professor. My point is, your philosophical premise is flawed to start with, and so your conclusion must also be flawed.'

The professor's face cannot hide his surprise this time. 'Flawed? Can you explain how?'

'You are working on the premise of duality,' the student explains. 'You argue that there is life and then there's death; a good God and a bad God. You are viewing the concept of God as something finite, something we can *measure. Sir, science can't even explain a thought.'* 'It uses electricity and magnetism, but has never seen, much less fully understood either one. To view death as the opposite of life is to be ignorant of the fact that death cannot exist as a substantive thing. Death is not the opposite of life, just the absence of it.' 'Now tell me, professor. Do you teach your students that they evolved from a monkey?'

'If you are referring to the natural evolutionary process, young man, yes, of course I do.'

'Have you ever observed evolution with your own eyes, sir?'

The professor begins to shake his head, still smiling, as he realizes where the argument is going. A very good semester, indeed.

'Since no one has ever observed the process of evolution at work and cannot even prove that this process is an on-going endeavor, are you not teaching your opinion, sir? Are you now not a scientist, but a preacher?'

The class is in uproar. The student remains silent until the commotion has subsided. 'To continue the point you were making earlier to the other student, let me give you an example of what I mean.' The student looks around the room. 'Is there anyone in the class who has ever seen the professor's brain?' The class breaks out into laughter. 'Is there anyone here who has ever heard the professor's brain, felt the professor's brain, touched or smelt the professor's brain? No one appears to have done so... So, according to the established rules of empirical, stable, demonstrable protocol, science says that you have no brain, with all due respect, sir.' 'So if science says you have no brain, how can we trust your lectures, sir?'

Now the room is silent. The professor just stares at the student, his face unreadable. Finally, after what seems an eternity, the old man answers. 'I guess you'll have to take them on faith.'

'Now, you accept that there is faith, and, in fact, faith exists with life,' the student continues. 'Now, sir, is there such a thing as evil?' Now uncertain, the professor responds, 'Of course, there is. We see it every day. It is in the daily *example of man's inhumanity to man. It is in the multitude of crime and violence everywhere in the world. These manifestations are nothing else but evil.'*

To this the student replied, 'Evil does not exist sir, or at least it does not exist unto itself. Evil is simply the absence of God. It is just like darkness and cold, a word that man has created to describe the absence of God. God did not create evil. Evil is the result of what happens when man does not have God's love present in his heart It's like the cold that comes when there is no heat or the darkness that comes when there is no light.'

The professor sat down.

PS: The student was Albert Einstein. Albert Einstein wrote a book titled 'God vs. Science' in 1921....

Recently a new movie was released entitled "God is Not Dead". The movie is based on the same premise as our story and in the climactic scene our hero (the student) wins the argument with the villain (the professor) by stating that "faith" is the proof of God. Each of us must come to personal decision regarding if God exists. If you have reached this point in reading and have decided that God does not exist, than further reading will not be of any help to you. It is not my intention, nor does it lie within my ability to convince you that God exists. I believe through faith that God does exist. This is a basic statement of who I am and what I believe. The rest of this book is an attempt to explain the why of salvation, the how of salvation, and the method of salvation. It is, however impossible to accept the premise of this book if you do not believe in God. If there is no God, then this book is a fairy tale and totally unnecessary for our lives.

If you have accepted the existence of God, than we can begin our journey as to what salvation is and both why God desires it and why we need it. Once we have accepted the concept that God does exist, then we must try to determine how He communicates with us. To this purpose we will use the BIBLE as our handbook of communication from God to mankind. When I was in college a professor described the Bible as mankind's attempt to communicate with a creator. It was years before I discovered just how wrong he was. The Bible is not a book of mankind reaching out to God, but rather a book describing how the Creator strives to reach out to mankind to bring them back into a personal relationship. In order to begin to understand this concept we will need to look at several passages the Bible uses to express this relationship.

We will first turn to the very beginning of the Bible. In Genesis 1:1-2 we find:

> *"IN the beginning God created the heaven and the earth. And the earth was without form, and void; and darkness was upon the face of the deep. And the Spirit of God moved upon the face of the waters."*

In the fourth word we find that it is God who is the Creator of the all things. This will be our guiding principle in seeking to understand God and His relationship to us. In John's gospel (John1:1-5) we also find these words:

> *"IN the beginning was the Word, and the Word was with God, and the Word was God. The same was in the beginning with God. All things were made by him; and without him was not any thing made that was made. In him was life; and the life was the light of men. And the light shineth in darkness; and the darkness comprehended it not."*

These words reflect the same basic concept as Genesis. The name "Word" used here is the Greek word "logos". Its meaning is more than just word. The meaning is the "truth of the matter" or "knowledge". John was attempting to explain that Christ was God and that he held the truth and knowledge. John was showing that the trinity created and was existent at the time the earth was created. It is the same concept that is used in Genesis when we see stated *"God created the heaven and earth"*. So we see that in both the old and new testaments the concept that God created everything is the basis for the books and our faith.

Once we have accepted a creator, then and only then can we begin to move on to explore the why of creation. Without an acceptance of a Creator, there is no need to go further. The reader having reached this point and accepted the fact of creation, is now prepared to move on to the why of creation.

I propose that first we look at why God established the process and why God desires it, and then how it is applied to us. In the next chapter we will look at why God created mankind.

CHAPTER 2
WHY MAN   WHY SALVATION

In order to understand salvation we must first understand the why. Why would God care about mankind or about the salvation of mankind? Does an almighty God need mankind, and does He need to provide for his salvation?

These questions form the whole basis of religion. If you have gotten to this point you have accepted that there is a God, who is the all-powerful creator of all things. Religion attempts to understand and explain the relationship between mankind and his Creator. We must at least attempt to answer the questions above if we are to have any hope of understanding the concept of salvation. Let's see if we can break these concepts into small enough pieces that we can attempt to explain them and understand them.

WHY MAN

The ultimate question. Why man? Why would the Creator chose mankind for this special role? We need only look to the very first book of the Bible to find the answer to this question. In Genesis 1:26-28 we find these words:

> *"And God said, Let us make man in our image, after our likeness: and let them have dominion over the fish of the sea, and over the fowl of the air, and over the cattle, and over all the earth, and over every creeping thing that creepeth upon the earth. So God created man in his own image, in the image of God created he him; male and female created he them. And God blessed them, and God said unto them, Be fruitful, and multiply, and replenish the earth, and subdue it: and have dominion over the fish of the sea, and over the fowl of the air, and over every living thing that moveth upon the earth."*

The reason that mankind was chosen, is that God created mankind to fill a special purpose in creation. We were a part of the plan from the very beginning. The decision was made before we were created that we would be made in the very image of God. This does not mean that we will all look like God, but rather that we would be the only creation that would have some of the aspects of God. Mankind alone of all of God's creation has the ability to choose (free will). Mankind was created to be a partner to God in ruling the earth. Adam was allowed to name every creature, and God built a beautiful garden for Adam to live in. It was to be Adam's job to keep the garden neat, and rule over the animals. We also read this in Genesis 1:29–31:

> "And God said, Behold, I have given you every herb bearing seed, which is upon the face of all the earth, and every tree, in the which is the fruit of a tree yielding seed; to you it shall be for meat. And to every beast of the earth, and to every fowl of the air, and to every thing that creepeth upon the earth, wherein there is life, I have given every green herb for meat: and it was so. And God saw every thing that he had made, and, behold, it was very good. And the evening and the morning were the sixth day."

Notice, that God outlines both specific privileges and responsibilities for Adam. God has given mankind an opportunity to exercise his free will over the earth and the inhabitants of the earth. To ensure mankind's happiness God created a companion for Adam and placed her in the garden as well. The story of mankind's creation is retold in the second chapter of Genesis (Genesis 2:18–25):

> "And the LORD God said, It is not good that the man should be alone; I will make him an help meet for him. And out of the ground the LORD God formed every beast of the field, and every fowl of the air; and brought them unto Adam to see what he would call them: and whatsoever Adam called every living creature, that was the name thereof. And Adam gave names to all cattle, and to the fowl of the air, and to every beast of the field; but for Adam there was not found an help meet for him. And the LORD God caused a deep sleep to fall upon Adam, and he slept: and he took one of his ribs, and closed up the flesh instead thereof; And the rib, which the LORD God had taken from man, made he a woman, and brought her unto the man. And Adam said, This is now bone of my bones, and flesh of my flesh: she shall be called Woman, because she was taken out of Man. Therefore shall a man leave his father and his mother,

and shall cleave unto his wife: and they shall be one flesh. And they were both naked, the man and his wife, and were not ashamed."

Here we find Adam naming the animals and establishing his place of dominance over all the other living creatures in the garden.

As we read the first two chapters of Genesis, we see that God structured the universe to suit His own purposes. Mankind becomes the highlight of that creation. Mankind was created to be the link between God and His creation. Mankind, alone, has the ability to reason, make his own decisions, and choose his own course. Creation is fully developed, and mankind is now placed in charge. As we continue our search, we will see God interact with His creation. The next question, is if all is well, why do we need salvation?

WHY SALVATION

As the second chapter of Genesis ends, we find a universe in harmony, with all of God's creations in place and living in peace. What happens that changes all of this. In the third chapter of Genesis (Genesis 3:1–24), we find our answer.

"Now the serpent was more subtil than any beast of the field which the LORD God had made. And he said unto the woman, Yea, hath God said, Ye shall not eat of every tree of the garden? And the woman said unto the serpent, We may eat of the fruit of the trees of the garden: But of the fruit of the tree which is in the midst of the garden, God hath said, Ye shall not eat of it, neither shall ye touch it, lest ye die. And the serpent said unto the woman, Ye shall not surely die: For God doth know that in the day ye eat thereof, then your eyes shall be opened, and ye shall be as gods, knowing good and evil. And when the woman saw that the tree was good for food, and that it was pleasant to the eyes, and a tree to be desired to make one wise, she took of the fruit thereof, and did eat, and gave also unto her husband with her; and he did eat. And the eyes of them both were opened, and they knew that they were naked; and they sewed fig leaves together, and

made themselves aprons. And they heard the voice of the Lord God walking in the garden in the cool of the day: and Adam and his wife hid themselves from the presence of the Lord God amongst the trees of the garden. And the Lord God called unto Adam, and said unto him, Where art thou? And he said, I heard thy voice in the garden, and I was afraid, because I was naked; and I hid myself. And he said, Who told thee that thou wast naked? Hast thou eaten of the tree, whereof I commanded thee that thou shouldest not eat? And the man said, The woman whom thou gavest to be with me, she gave me of the tree, and I did eat. And the Lord God said unto the woman, What is this that thou hast done? And the woman said, The serpent beguiled me, and I did eat. And the Lord God said unto the serpent, Because thou hast done this, thou art cursed above all cattle, and above every beast of the field; upon thy belly shalt thou go, and dust shalt thou eat all the days of thy life: And I will put enmity between thee and the woman, and between thy seed and her seed; it shall bruise thy head, and thou shalt bruise his heel. Unto the woman he said, I will greatly multiply thy sorrow and thy conception; in sorrow thou shalt bring forth children; and thy desire shall be to thy husband, and he shall rule over thee. And unto Adam he said, Because thou hast hearkened unto the voice of thy wife, and hast eaten of the tree, of which I commanded thee, saying, Thou shalt not eat of it: cursed is the ground for thy sake; in sorrow shalt thou eat of it all the days of thy life; Thorns also and thistles shall it bring forth to thee; and thou shalt eat the herb of the field; In the sweat of thy face shalt thou eat bread, till thou return unto the ground; for out of it wast thou taken: for dust thou art, and unto dust shalt thou return. And Adam called his wife's name Eve; because she was the mother of all living. Unto Adam also and to his wife did the Lord God make coats of skins, and clothed them. And the Lord God said, Behold, the man is become as one of us, to know good and evil: and now, lest he put forth his hand, and take also of the tree of life, and eat, and live for ever: Therefore the Lord God sent him forth from the garden of Eden, to till the ground from whence he was taken. So he drove out the man; and he placed at the east of the garden of Eden Cherubims, and a flaming sword which turned every way, to keep the way of the tree of life."

The quick answer to this is that man used the free will God had given him to rebel against God's will. Many people try to put the blame on Satan for the fall of man. This is simply not the truth. Satan for his own reasons tempted man to rebel, but could not compel man to rebel. It was through free will that first Eve and then Adam rebelled against God's will. I remember a TV show from the 70's in which Flip Wilson would do a skit in which he got in trouble. When asked why, his answer was *"the devil made me do it"*. If we are willing to confront the fact that we do have free will, then we are not allowed to say *"the devil made me do it"*. Recently I had a teenager tell me that she did not have free will, that her mother, teachers, other people made her do things she did not really want to do. My answer was, of course, that she did have free will, and the reason she did these things, was not because someone made her, but because by doing them she suffered less pain in her life. I told her, that she did indeed have free will, to do as she pleased, but that there were consequences to her actions. She was telling me that the consequences of obeying these people was less odious than disobeying them. Satan used this same reasoning, when he discussed God's rules with Eve. He tried to convince her that God did not really say what the rule was, and that if she disobeyed God that the punishment would be less than the pleasure received by disobeying. At no time did Satan command her to disobey God. As a matter of fact, we find in the book of Job (Job 1:6-7, 2:1-2)

> *"Now there was a day when the sons of God came to present themselves before the LORD, and Satan came also among them. And the LORD said unto Satan, Whence comest thou? Then Satan answered the LORD, and said, From going to and fro in the earth, and from walking up and down in it."*

> *"Again there was a day when the sons of God came to present themselves before the LORD, and Satan came also among them to present himself before the LORD. And the LORD said unto Satan, From whence comest thou? And Satan answered the LORD, and said, From going to and fro in the earth, and from walking up and down in it."*

We can see that God required that all of the angels report to Him on a regular basis. We also see that Satan was also required to be there and report to God. He could not choose to disobey God. Satan did NOT have free will, only Adam and Eve had free will. While Satan could entice them to disobey God, he could not command them to disobey.

By choosing to disobey God, Adam and Eve exercised free will. They both chose the act and were forced to accept the consequences. After disobeying God, they felt the remorse, and tried to hide their nakedness and themselves from God when He came to walk in the garden to commune with them. In chapter 2 (Genesis 2:16–17):

> *"And the LORD God commanded the man, saying, Of every tree of the garden thou mayest freely eat: But of the tree of the knowledge of good and evil, thou shalt not eat of it: for in the day that thou eatest thereof thou shalt surely die."*

We find the exact nature of their rebellion. God had commanded that they not eat the fruit of a certain tree in the middle of the garden. Both Adam and Eve ate the fruit, as thus disobeyed God. Satan told Eve that she would not die if she ate the fruit, and as we can see she does not immediately die from eating the fruit. Some sceptics of the Bible use this as proof that the Bible is not true. They like Satan merely do not understand the Bible. God did not say that Eve would die immediately, but that she would of a certainty die. It was not God's plan for Adam and Eve to die. His plan was that they would live forever. Death was the consequence of their sin. Now they would surely die, not immediately, but they would die. God allowed them to live their lives, so that they might have a chance to change and obtain salvation.

As a result of their sin, Adam and Eve both were forced to accept the punishment for their sins. God's first act was to verify their sin, by asking them if they had broken His commandment. Adam answers first, and like the rest of us when we are caught, Adam tries to pawn off the blame on Eve. Eve follows Adam's example and tries to pawn off the blame on Satan. Notice that God answers in the opposite order with the punishment. First God tells Satan that He will be force to live as the serpent, and that while he may bruise the Saviour's heal, the Saviour will bruise Satan's head. This is a very important verse. God is telling Satan that there will be a Saviour, and that the Saviour will be a child of Eve. Further, God is telling Satan, that the Saviour will be responsible for his downfall. We can see, that even from the very beginning of Genesis and mankind, that God has a plan in place to bring redemption to the world.

As we can see in Genesis 4:1:

"Adam knew Eve his wife; and she conceived, and bare Cain, and said, I have gotten a man from the LORD."

Eve understood the message and proudly stated that she had "gotten a man from the Lord". Eve believed that Cain would be the Saviour who would redeem her from her sins.

God next proclaims Eve's punishment in that she would be subject to her husband and bear her children in pain. God further stated that her desire would be toward her husband. Finally God pronounces judgment upon Adam. Adam was to till the land in sorrow, and be faced with thorns thistles. By sweat would Adam grow and make his bread all of his days until he died.

Finally God began teaching Adam and Eve about the plan of salvation. God killed an animal and made clothing for both Adam and Eve. The example for them was that there must be a sacrifice and blood shed as the result of sin. God also used the killing of the animal to introduce the concept of sacrifice to them. I believe God also instructed them in the manner of the sacrifice. We can see this in the fact that both Cain and Able, when they were old enough brought sacrifices to God. Finally God removed them from Eden and placed them in the world to live out their lives.

As we have learned, disobedience brought sin into the world, and there is a price to be paid for that disobedience. The plan has been formed and God is now teaching mankind how to follow the plan until it is fulfilled and redemption is brought to the world.

Before we leave this and begin our actual exploration of the plan of salvation, we need to finish this account of the fall of mankind, and God's initial instructions as He moves us to redemption. In Genesis 4:1-7:

"And Adam knew Eve his wife; and she conceived, and bare Cain, and said, I have gotten a man from the LORD. And she again bare his brother Abel. And Abel was a keeper of sheep, but Cain was a tiller of the ground. And in process of time it came to pass, that Cain brought of the fruit of the ground an offering unto the LORD. And Abel, he also brought of the firstlings of his flock and of the fat thereof. And the LORD had respect unto Abel and to his offering: But unto Cain and to

> *his offering he had not respect. And Cain was very wroth, and his countenance fell. And the LORD said unto Cain, Why art thou wroth? and why is thy countenance fallen? If thou doest well, shalt thou not be accepted? and if thou doest not well, sin lieth at the door. And unto thee shall be his desire, and thou shalt rule over him."*

We find mankind practicing the instructions they received from God concerning the sacrifice. We see the two brothers each bringing a sacrifice from their own particular area of interest. Cain brings a sacrifice from the things that he had grown and Abel from the first fruits of his flock. As we follow this account, we find that God did not accept Cain's offering, but did accept Abel's offering. I have read numerous explanations as to why God refused Cain's offering. The most prominent of these is that it was not a blood sacrifice. The theory was that God had commanded a blood offering and Cain failed to provide one. Why would Cain even attempt an offering of his crops, if he was taught that only a blood sacrifice would be accepted? As we look at God's conversation with Cain, we find that God told Cain his offering would be accepted if he did well. God was telling Cain that he needed a change in attitude if he wanted God to accept his offering. I believe that Cain brought his offering out of duty and begrudgingly. This was a perverted attempt by Cain to impose his will on God's commandment. Cain's theory was that he could make the rules himself. Cain believed it was just a ritual, something he had to do to keep God off his back. God did not want an offering made by ritual, but rather an offering made out of honor and respect. God told Cain He would accept any offering made out of respect, but no matter how good the offering, it would not be accepted if it was done begrudgingly.

> *"And Cain was very wroth, and his countenance fell. And the LORD said unto Cain, Why art thou wroth? and why is thy countenance fallen? If thou doest well, shalt thou not be accepted? and if thou doest not well, sin lieth at the door. And unto thee shall be his desire, and thou shalt rule over him."*

Follow what the Bible says. God told Cain to do well and his offering would be accepted, but that if Cain continued with his attitude, that sin would follow him and rule over him. We can still see that today in the lives of some people. They place their own desires above dong what is right, and often fall into a lifestyle that brings death and destruction to them.

As we follow the account (Genesis 4:8-16):

> *"And Cain talked with Abel his brother: and it came to pass, when they were in the field, that Cain rose up against Abel his brother, and slew him. And the LORD said unto Cain, Where is Abel thy brother? And he said, I know not: Am I my brother's keeper? And he said, What hast thou done? the voice of thy brother's blood crieth unto me from the ground. And now art thou cursed from the earth, which hath opened her mouth to receive thy brother's blood from thy hand; When thou tillest the ground, it shall not henceforth yield unto thee her strength; a fugitive and a vagabond shalt thou be in the earth. And Cain said unto the LORD, My punishment is greater than I can bear. Behold, thou hast driven me out this day from the face of the earth; and from thy face shall I be hid; and I shall be a fugitive and a vagabond in the earth; and it shall come to pass, that every one that findeth me shall slay me. And the LORD said unto him, Therefore whosoever slayeth Cain, vengeance shall be taken on him sevenfold. And the LORD set a mark upon Cain, lest any finding him should kill him. And Cain went out from the presence of the LORD, and dwelt in the land of Nod, on the east of Eden."*

We see that Cain did indeed fall into that pit that leads to destruction. Cain could not take out his frustration on God, so he turned to Abel and placed the blame on him. I am sure that Abel tried to instruct Cain in the right way, and this probably made Cain that much madder because he knew that Abel was right. Being right can be a dangerous thing. Cain kills his brother and when confronted by God, his only answer is *"Am I my brother's keeper"*. Just like his parents, Cain tries to remove the blame from himself. God judges Cain and pronounces that judgment to him immediately. Cain pleads that the judgment is too harsh and tells God he will be killed by anyone who meets him. God informs Cain that His judgment will be seven fold on anyone who kills Cain, and places a mark on Cain so that everyone knows who he is and what he has done. God chose to not kill Cain, but to make him an example of what sin can do in a person's life. We can see that God is continuing to instruct mankind in correct behavior toward both God and their fellow man.

We can understand from these two accounts, that God has rules that must be obeyed, and that there is a price to be paid for disobedience. We can also see that God has made plans for the redemption of man and made the promise to Eve that one of her descendants would bring that redemption.

We can now see why mankind was chosen, and why we need salvation. All that is left is to determine what God's plan of salvation is and how it was accomplished. To look ahead, in the next paragraph we can see that mankind has been informed of the plan and understands the plan God has created.

We know the message of salvation was known from the account we can follow in the book of Job. The account of Job is the oldest recorded account in the Bible. It is believed to have been written about the time of Abraham and talks of the time of the patriarchs. In Job 19:25 we find these words:

"For I know that my redeemer liveth, And that he shall stand at the latter day upon the earth:"

Job, uses the word redeemer to describe the person who will bring salvation to him. The Hebrew root word used here is translated as both "redeemer" and "kinsman redeemer" in the Old Testament. The concept of redemption is tied the concept of a kinsman. As we begin to look for the explanation of this concept, we will see how the Bible brings all of this together with the Christ's walk to the cross.

In the following chapters we will explore this concept and see why Christ is our kinsman redeemer.

CHAPTER 3
SACRIFICE
ADAM

In order to fully understand the subject of salvation, it will be necessary for us to look at two separate doctrines (truths) that are demonstrated in the Bible. In this chapter we will look at the doctrine of sacrifice, and in the next chapter the doctrine of the Kinsman Redeemer. As we have already seen, sacrifice was first practiced in the Garden of Eden. As we read in Genesis 3:21:

> "Unto Adam also and to his wife did the LORD God make coats of skins, and clothed them."

God makes the first sacrifice of an animal in order to make clothing for Adam and Eve. As you will recall, when they sinned, they tried to cover themselves with leaves. Since this will not be practical as they enter the world, God creates clothing for them out of animal skins. Adam and Eve would not have been able to do this, since they have never experienced death. At this point in the world, Adam and Eve did not eat meat. It is not until after the flood that animals as food enters into the world. I believe that at this point God instructed Adam and Eve in the need for and practice of sacrifice. We can see that it has become a standard practice by the time that Cain and Abel have become men. In Genesis 4:3–4:

> "And in process of time it came to pass, that Cain brought of the fruit of the ground an offering unto the LORD. And Abel, he also brought of the firstlings of his flock and of the fat thereof. And the LORD had respect unto Abel and to his offering."

We can see that both of Adam's sons brought a sacrifice to God. It should be evident that Adam and Eve had told them the story of their sin and described the nature of the sacrifice that would be required of them to cover their sin.

NOAH

The history of sacrifice can easily be followed and mankind's story unfolds in the Bible. The next occurrence of sacrifice is found in Genesis 7:2–9:

> "Of every clean beast thou shalt take to thee by sevens, the male and his female: and of beasts that are not clean by two, the male and his female. Of fowls also of the air by sevens, the male and the female; to keep seed alive upon the face of all the earth. For yet seven days, and I will cause it to rain upon the earth forty days and forty nights; and every living substance that I have made will I destroy from off the face of the earth. And Noah did according unto all that the LORD commanded him. And Noah was six hundred years old when the flood of waters was upon the earth. And Noah went in, and his sons, and his wife, and his sons' wives with him, into the ark, because of the waters of the flood. Of clean beasts, and of beasts that are not clean, and of fowls, and of every thing that creepeth upon the earth,"

Whoa, wait a minute, this is not about sacrifice, it is about clean and unclean animals. That is exactly correct. From this passage, we can increase our knowledge as to what the requirements were for the sacrifice. Not all animals we desirable for the sacrifice. Only certain animals were allowed for the sacrifice. Remember mankind has a vegetarian diet at this point. The only reason for taking more than two of each animal would be for the sacrifice. These were not food animals, but sacrificial animals. The need to take seven pairs of these clean animals were so that there would be animals available for the sacrifice. We are not told exactly which animals were clean and which were unclean, but we will discover this later in our research. Now that we understand how there were animals to sacrifice after the flood, we can look to the sacrifice itself. After the waters have receded, and Noah has left the ark his first task is to build an altar and make the sacrifice. Genesis 8:20 records this:

> "And Noah builded an altar unto the LORD; and took of every clean beast, and of every clean fowl, and offered burnt offerings on the altar."

The first thing that Noah does is to make a sacrifice to God to thank God for saving his life and the lives of his family. From this we can learn how important the sacrifice was to Noah and his family. We can also learn that God made the provision for this by increasing the number of clean animals on the ark, so that there would be an animal for the sacrifice. It should be noted here that we are now about fifteen hundred (1500) years from creation. Sacrifice is an established part of mankind's heritage. The practice of sacrifice has been a part of life for over 1500 years. It should be evident from this that all of mankind both knew and practiced sacrifice. Noah is continuing the practice after the flood and instructing his sons in the correct method. As we move forward in time we can follow the results of this instruction.

ABRAHAM

Our next account of sacrifice is the account of Abram being called out to found the Hebrew nation. We find there are several verses in Genesis that show Abram understood the concept of sacrifice and practiced it as part of his worship of God. We will start with the first mention of Abram in Genesis 12:7:

> *"And the LORD appeared unto Abram, and said, Unto thy seed will I give this land: and there builded he an altar unto the LORD, who appeared unto him."*

As soon as God appears to Abram, he stops and builds an altar to commemorate the appearance of God, and to honor God for the blessing he receives. This continues in the next chapter of Genesis with Abram returning to the altar he had built, after he strayed into Egypt and left the blessing that had been promised. Also, during this time we have no record of any sacrifices by Abram. Upon returning to the land God had chosen for him, Abram again returns to the sacrifices that God had commanded. This is an act of repentance to God to signify that Abram understood the failing and wished to return to the blessing that God had promised him. (Genesis 13:4)

> *"Unto the place of the altar, which he had made there at the first: and there Abram called on the name of the LORD."*

We can now see that Abram is faithful in following God, because when he moved his tent to a new area, he stops to build another altar to God to insure he could worship in the new area. (Genesis 13:18)

> *"Then Abram removed his tent, and came and dwelt in the plain of Mamre, which is in Hebron, and built there an altar unto the LORD."*

In Genesis 15:1-17 we find that Abram claims the promise made to him by God and requests that God fulfill the promise of making Abram a great nation, by giving him a son. God tells Abram to make a sacrifice of a heifer of three years old, and a she goat of three years old, and a ram of three years old, and a turtledove, and a young pigeon. Abram is faithful to do this and to watch over the sacrifice until dark. When the darkness comes Abram falls into a deep sleep and God informs him that his children will be in captivity for over 400 years, but that they will return to the land God has given them and become a great people. After this God sends the fire to consume the sacrifice to prove the power of His word.

> *"After these things the word of the LORD came unto Abram in a vision, saying, Fear not, Abram: I am thy shield, and thy exceeding great reward. And Abram said, Lord GOD, what wilt thou give me, seeing I go childless, and the steward of my house is this Eliezer of Damascus? And Abram said, Behold, to me thou hast given no seed: and, lo, one born in my house is mine heir. And, behold, the word of the LORD came unto him, saying, This shall not be thine heir; but he that shall come forth out of thine own bowels shall be thine heir. And he brought him forth abroad, and said, Look now toward heaven, and tell the stars, if thou be able to number them: and he said unto him, So shall thy seed be. And he believed in the LORD; and he counted it to him for righteousness. And he said unto him, I am the LORD that brought thee out of Ur of the Chaldees, to give thee this land to inherit it. And he said, Lord GOD, whereby shall I know that I shall inherit it? And he said unto him, Take me an heifer of three years old, and a she goat of three years old, and a ram of three years old, and a turtledove, and a young pigeon. And he took unto him all these, and divided them in the midst, and laid each piece one against another: but the birds divided he not. And when the fowls came down upon the carcases, Abram drove them away.*

> *And when the sun was going down, a deep sleep fell upon Abram; and, lo, an horror of great darkness fell upon him. And he said unto Abram, Know of a surety that thy seed shall be a stranger in a land that is not theirs, and shall serve them; and they shall afflict them four hundred years; And also that nation, whom they shall serve, will I judge: and afterward shall they come out with great substance. And thou shalt go to thy fathers in peace; thou shalt be buried in a good old age. But in the fourth generation they shall come hither again: for the iniquity of the Amorites is not yet full. And it came to pass, that, when the sun went down, and it was dark, behold a smoking furnace, and a burning lamp that passed between those pieces."*

We are now introduced to the next and perhaps the most important lesson of sacrifice. Up until this point mankind has sacrificed animals to cover their sins. Now we will see that Abraham will be asked to sacrifice a human, and not just any human, but his only son. Remember, Abraham is relying on his son Isaac to found the great nation that God has promised Abraham. Follow the story as it unfolds, and we will be able to see the next step in our education of the purpose of sacrifice. The story unfolds in Genesis 22:1-18:

> *"And it came to pass after these things, that God did tempt Abraham, and said unto him, Abraham: and he said, Behold, here I am. and he said, Take now thy son, thine only son Isaac, whom thou lovest, and get thee into the land of Moriah; and offer him there for a burnt offering upon one of the mountains which I will tell thee of. And Abraham rose up early in the morning, and saddled his ass, and took two of his young men with him, and Isaac his son, and clave the wood for the burnt offering, and rose up, and went unto the place of which God had told him. Then on the third day Abraham lifted up his eyes, and saw the place afar off. And Abraham said unto his young men, Abide ye here with the ass; and I and the lad will go yonder and worship, and come again to you. And Abraham took the wood of the burnt offering, and laid it upon Isaac his son; and he took the fire in his hand, and a knife; and they went both of them together. And Isaac spake unto Abraham his*

*father, and said, My father: and he said, Here am I, my son. And he said, Behold the fire and the wood: but where is the lamb for a burnt offering? And Abraham said, My son, God will provide himself a lamb for a burnt offering: so they went both of them together. And they came to the place which God had told him of; and Abraham built an altar there, and laid the wood in order, and bound Isaac his son, and laid him on the altar upon the wood. And Abraham stretched forth his hand, and took the knife to slay his son. And the angel of the L*ORD *called unto him out of heaven, and said, Abraham, Abraham: and he said, Here am I. And he said, Lay not thine hand upon the lad, neither do thou any thing unto him: for now I know that thou fearest God, seeing thou hast not withheld thy son, thine only son from me. And Abraham lifted up his eyes, and looked, and behold behind him a ram caught in a thicket by his horns: and Abraham went and took the ram, and offered him up for a burnt offering in the stead of his son. And Abraham called the name of that place Jehovah-jireh: as it is said to this day, In the mount of the L*ORD *it shall be seen. And the angel of the L*ORD *called unto Abraham out of heaven the second time, And said, By myself have I sworn, saith the L*ORD*, for because thou hast done this thing, and hast not withheld thy son, thine only son: That in blessing I will bless thee, and in multiplying I will multiply thy seed as the stars of the heaven, and as the sand which is upon the sea shore; and thy seed shall possess the gate of his enemies; And in thy seed shall all the nations of the earth be blessed; because thou hast obeyed my voice."*

Abraham is called by God to make a sacrifice. He is told where to go and Abraham immediately begins making preparations for the journey. He calls to his son Isaac and a couple of his servants to prepare for the journey. They load up animals with the wood for the sacrifice and the supplies they will need on the trip and set out for the site God has commanded. After a three day journey they reach the area of the sacrifice. Abraham tells the servants to wait for him here, and Abraham and Isaac continue on to the place of the sacrifice. Abraham does not allow his servants to continue, because God has told him he must make a sacrifice of Isaac, his only son, and Abraham does not want them to interfere with what is to happen.

We must make note of several things happening that are unique to this particular sacrifice. The first thing we notice, is that for the first time God has required a human sacrifice. God has never required a human sacrifice before. In fact God has punished mankind for taking human life. Now God is requiring a human sacrifice. Not only is it a human sacrifice, but a particular human to be sacrificed. Isaac, Abraham's only son is to be sacrificed. It is important to remember Abraham's age when Isaac is born. Abraham and Sarah are old when Isaac is born, and the chance of having another child is probably behind them. God has informed Abraham that he will become a great nation through the children of Isaac. Now God is removing Isaac from the scene. What will happen to the promise God made to Abraham.

The next fact we observe is that Abraham is obedient to God. Knowing what is to happen, Abraham still follows God's request and takes Isaac to be sacrificed. As Abraham and Isaac leave the servants, Abraham binds Isaac to the wood on his back. Many theologians claim this a foreshadowing of Christ being bound to the wood of the cross. Abraham takes the fire and the knife, and they proceed to the place of the sacrifice. We also see that Isaac is obedient to his father in following him to the place of the sacrifice.

On the path to the place of the sacrifice, Isaac asks Abraham a question. Where is the lamb for the sacrifice? Abraham, in a great statement of faith in God, replies that *"My son, God will provide himself a lamb for a burnt offering:"* There is no question that this is a reference to the cross and the sacrifice of Christ on that cross. God is now for the first time instructing mankind in the manner in which salvation will be obtained. Salvation will require the blood sacrifice of a human. Not only a human, but a human who meets the requirement of the animal sacrifice. The human must be pure and without blemish. For the first time God is revealing that salvation will come through a blood sacrifice. There is no doubt, that Abraham believed that God would require him to sacrifice the child that he loved, his only child. Abraham was faithful to God and proceeded to build the altar, place the wood on the altar, and bind his son to the altar in order to slay him for the sacrifice.

At the last minute we see the angel of the Lord appears and stops the slaying of Isaac. In Old Testament Biblical language, the angel of the

Lord is used to refer to the Christ. Here long before he is born, the Christ appears to stop the sacrifice of Isaac. Abraham has proved his worth and faithfulness by being ready to sacrifice Isaac. At the same time God has given us a foreshadowing of the death of Christ. We have learned what will be required for our salvation. All that is left is for the sacrifice to take place. In fulfillment of the words of Abraham, they see a ram tangled in the thicket. This animal prepared and provided by God is now sacrificed on the altar.

The next lesson in the history of sacrifice had been delivered to mankind. Sin will require a human sacrifice. Also we have yet to be told the requirements of the human sacrifice. These facts were know by Abraham and everyone else at that time, but have not yet been recorded in the Bible for our instruction.

MOSES

We must follow along in the Bible to the next lesson to learn more of the requirements of the sacrifice. We will now move another 400 plus years into the history of Israel for our next lesson. It will be necessary for us to look at Moses and the Passover for our next lesson. This is a well-known story of how Moses returned to Egypt and instructed the Pharaoh to let Israel leave. Of course Pharaoh refused and Egypt was forced to endure nine plagues up to the point where will pick up the story in the Bible. It is important to note that the first nine plagues were not a useless preview of what was to come. Egypt had many gods, and the nine plagues were each directed to a particular god. God was teaching Egypt that their gods could not save them and were useless in preventing God from fulfilling His plan. As each of the nine plagues unfolds a particular god of Egypt is struck down and discredited. The only god left is Pharaoh himself. The tenth plague is directed against Pharaoh himself. The sun god Ra as represented by Pharaoh will be struck down as the firstborn of Egypt, including Pharaoh's son will be destroyed. The account is told in Exodus 11–12:

> *"And the LORD said unto Moses, Yet will I bring one plague more upon Pharaoh, and upon Egypt; afterwards he will let you go hence: when he shall let you go, he shall surely thrust*

you out hence altogether. Speak now in the ears of the people, and let every man borrow of his neighbour, and every woman of her neighbour, jewels of silver, and jewels of gold. And the LORD *gave the people favour in the sight of the Egyptians. Moreover the man Moses was very great in the land of Egypt, in the sight of Pharaoh's servants, and in the sight of the people. And Moses said, Thus saith the* LORD, *About midnight will I go out into the midst of Egypt: And all the firstborn in the land of Egypt shall die, from the firstborn of Pharaoh that sitteth upon his throne, even unto the firstborn of the maidservant that is behind the mill; and all the firstborn of beasts. And there shall be a great cry throughout all the land of Egypt, such as there was none like it, nor shall be like it any more. But against any of the children of Israel shall not a dog move his tongue, against man or beast: that ye may know how that the* LORD *doth put a difference between the Egyptians and Israel. And all these thy servants shall come down unto me, and bow down themselves unto me, saying, Get thee out, and all the people that follow thee: and after that I will go out. And he went out from Pharaoh in a great anger. And the* LORD *said unto Moses, Pharaoh shall not hearken unto you; that my wonders may be multiplied in the land of Egypt. And Moses and Aaron did all these wonders before Pharaoh: and the* LORD *hardened Pharaoh's heart, so that he would not let the children of Israel go out of his land.*

And the LORD *spake unto Moses and Aaron in the land of Egypt, saying, This month shall be unto you the beginning of months: it shall be the first month of the year to you. Speak ye unto all the congregation of Israel, saying, In the tenth day of this month they shall take to them every man a lamb, according to the house of their fathers, a lamb for an house: And if the household be too little for the lamb, let him and his neighbour next unto his house take it according to the number of the souls; every man according to his eating shall make your count for the lamb. Your lamb shall be without blemish, a male of the first year: ye shall take it out from the sheep, or from the goats: And ye shall keep it up until the fourteenth day of the same month: and the whole assembly of the congregation of Israel shall kill it in the evening. And they shall take of the blood, and strike it on the two side posts and on the upper door post of the houses, wherein they shall eat it. And they shall eat the flesh in that night, roast with fire, and unleavened bread; and with bitter herbs they shall eat it. Eat not of it raw, nor sodden at all with water, but roast with fire; his head with his legs, and with the purtenance thereof. And ye shall let nothing of it remain until the morning; and that which remaineth of it until the morning ye shall burn with fire. And thus shall ye eat it; with your loins girded, your shoes on your feet, and your staff in your hand; and ye shall eat it in haste: it is the LORD's passover. For I will pass through the land of Egypt this night, and will smite all the firstborn in the land of Egypt, both man and beast; and against all the gods of Egypt I will execute judgment: I am the LORD. And the blood shall be to you for a token upon the houses where ye are: and when I see the blood, I will pass over you, and the plague shall not be upon you to destroy you, when I smite the land of Egypt. And this day shall be unto you for a memorial; and ye shall keep it a feast to the LORD throughout your generations; ye shall keep it a feast by an ordinance for ever. Seven days shall ye eat unleavened bread; even the first day ye shall put away leaven out of your houses: for whosoever eateth leavened bread from the first day until the seventh day, that soul shall be cut off from Israel. And in the first day there shall be an holy convocation, and in the seventh day there shall be an holy convocation to you; no manner of work shall be done in them, save that which every man must eat, that only may be done of you. And ye shall observe the feast of unleavened bread; for in this selfsame day have I brought your armies out of the land of Egypt: therefore shall ye observe this day in your generations by an ordinance for ever. In the first month, on the fourteenth day of the month at even, ye shall eat unleavened bread, until the one and twentieth day of the month at even. Seven days shall there be no leaven found in your houses: for whosoever eateth that which is leavened, even that soul shall be cut off from the congregation of Israel, whether he be a stranger, or born in the land. Ye shall eat nothing leavened; in all your habitations shall ye eat unleavened bread.*

Then Moses called for all the elders of Israel, and said unto them, Draw out and take you a lamb according to your families, and kill the passover. And ye shall take a bunch of hyssop, and dip it in the blood that is in the bason, and strike the lintel and the two side posts with the blood that is in the bason; and none of you shall go out at the door of his house until the morning. For the LORD will pass through to smite the Egyptians; and when he seeth the blood upon the lintel, and on the two side posts, the LORD will pass over the door, and will not suffer the destroyer to come in unto your houses to smite you. And ye shall observe this thing for an ordinance to thee and to thy sons for ever. And it shall come to pass, when ye be come to the land which the LORD will give you, according as he hath promised, that ye shall keep this service. And it shall come to pass, when your children shall say unto you, What mean ye by this service? That ye shall say, It is the sacrifice of the LORD's passover, who passed over the houses of the children of Israel in Egypt, when he smote the Egyptians, and delivered our houses. And the people bowed the head and worshipped. And the children of Israel went away, and did as the LORD had commanded Moses and Aaron, so did they.

And it came to pass, that at midnight the LORD smote all the firstborn in the land of Egypt, from the firstborn of Pharaoh that sat on his throne unto the firstborn of the captive that was in the dungeon; and all the firstborn of cattle. And Pharaoh rose up in the night, he, and all his servants, and all the Egyptians; and there was a great cry in Egypt; for there was not a house where there was not one dead. And he called for Moses and Aaron by night, and said, Rise up, and get you forth from among my people, both ye and the children of Israel; and go, serve the LORD, as ye have said. Also take your flocks and your herds, as ye have said, and be gone; and bless me also. And the Egyptians were urgent upon the people, that they might send them out of the land in haste; for they said, We be all dead men. And the people took their dough before it was leavened, their kneadingtroughs being bound up in their clothes upon their shoulders. And the children of Israel did according to the word of Moses; and they borrowed of the Egyptians jewels of silver, and jewels of gold, and raiment: And the LORD gave the people favour in the sight of the Egyptians, so that they lent unto them such things as they required. And they spoiled the Egyptians.

And the children of Israel journeyed from Rameses to Succoth, about six hundred thousand on foot that were men, beside children. And a mixed multitude went up also with them; and flocks, and herds, even very much cattle. And they baked unleavened cakes of the dough which they brought forth out of Egypt, for it was not leavened; because they were thrust out of Egypt, and could not tarry, neither had they prepared for themselves any victual. Now the sojourning of the children of Israel, who dwelt in Egypt, was four hundred and thirty years. And it came to pass at the end of the four hundred and thirty years, even the selfsame day it came to pass, that all the hosts of the LORD went out from the land of Egypt. It is a night to be much observed unto the LORD for bringing them out from the land of Egypt: this is that night of the LORD to be observed of all the children of Israel in their generations.

And the LORD said unto Moses and Aaron, This is the ordinance of the passover: There shall no stranger eat thereof: But every man's servant that is bought for money, when thou hast circumcised him, then shall he eat thereof. A foreigner and an hired servant shall not eat thereof. In one house shall it be eaten; thou shalt not carry forth ought of the flesh abroad out of the house; neither shall ye break a bone thereof. All the congregation of Israel shall keep it. And when a stranger shall sojourn with thee, and will keep the passover to the LORD, let all his males be circumcised, and then let him come near and keep it; and he shall be as one that is born in the land: for no uncircumcised person shall eat thereof. One law shall be to him that is homeborn, and unto the stranger that sojourneth among you. Thus did all the children of Israel; as the LORD commanded Moses and Aaron, so did

> *they. And it came to pass the selfsame day, that the LORD did bring the children of Israel out of the land of Egypt by their armies."*

As we pick up the account, God tells Moses that there will be one last plague against Egypt, and recounts the necessary steps Moses must take before the plague comes. Chapter 11 recalls these instructions to Moses. Moses is also told that Pharaoh will not listen to him and that the plague will happen. Moses is also told to prepare the people to leave after the tenth plague. The message in chapter 11 is that every first born in Egypt will die, but that all of Israel will be saved. In Exodus 11:7 we find these words:

> *"But against any of the children of Israel shall not a dog move his tongue, against man or beast: that ye may know how that the LORD doth put a difference between the Egyptians and Israel."*

Israel will be protected from the plague and will be allowed to leave to return to the Promised Land.

Chapter 12 gives us the account of the plague and the rules of sacrifice that Israel must follow as a result of the plague. We can know that this will be an important part of the instruction from that fact that God commands that Israel start a new calendar beginning in the month of the sacrifice and the last plague. It was a common custom in ancient times to begin a new calendar when an important event happened (i.e. the crowning of a new king etc.) God is telling Israel that this will become a new ritual in the practice of their worship of God. It has indeed become a new part of Jewish history and has now been celebrated for over 3,500 years. In Exodus 12:2 we find this:

> *"This month shall be unto you the beginning of months: it shall be the first month of the year to you."*

This now marks the event as special and Israel continues to this day to begin their calendar and year with this feast.

God next instructs Israel on how to celebrate the feast. In Exodus 12:3-11 God gives the instructions for the Passover:

> *"Speak ye unto all the congregation of Israel, saying, In the tenth day of this month they shall take to them every man a lamb, according to the house of their fathers, a lamb for an*

house: And if the household be too little for the lamb, let him and his neighbour next unto his house take it according to the number of the souls; every man according to his eating shall make your count for the lamb. Your lamb shall be without blemish, a male of the first year: ye shall take it out from the sheep, or from the goats: And ye shall keep it up until the fourteenth day of the same month: and the whole assembly of the congregation of Israel shall kill it in the evening. And they shall take of the blood, and strike it on the two side posts and on the upper door post of the houses, wherein they shall eat it. And they shall eat the flesh in that night, roast with fire, and unleavened bread; and with bitter herbs they shall eat it. Eat not of it raw, nor sodden at all with water, but roast with fire; his head with his legs, and with the purtenance thereof. And ye shall let nothing of it remain until the morning; and that which remaineth of it until the morning ye shall burn with fire. And thus shall ye eat it; with your loins girded, your shoes on your feet, and your staff in your hand; and ye shall eat it in haste: it is the LORD's passover.

    The requirement will be to take a perfect lamb of the size to feed just their family. If their family is too small for a lamb, they are to share a lamb with their neighbor. The perfect unblemished lamb is to be put up for two weeks, and then on the night of the Passover, the lamb is to be killed. The blood of the lamb is to be put on both sides and the top of the door. We are told later that this will be the sign God's angel will use to know which houses to spare. The lamb is to be roasted over the fire. The whole lamb was to be roasted whole, including the inner parts. It was not to be boiled or stewed, it was to be roasted over the fire. All of the lamb was to be eaten, and if anything was left in the morning, it was to be burned with the fire. Israel was also required to be dressed for a journey. They were to eat the lamb with unleavened bread, as there would not be time for the bread to rise. Israel needed to be ready to march in the morning. They would leave Egypt in the morning, after the angel of God had killed the first born of Egypt.

    In the rest of the chapter God instructs Israel of the importance of the feast. It will be for all time and will only be observed by Israel. They are not to allow a gentile to take part in the observance of the feast. It will be observed for all time as a symbol of God's deliverance of Israel from captivity in Egypt.

For the first time, we see that the blood has become more important than the sacrifice itself. It will be the blood on the door posts that save the firstborn of Israel. Remember that the firstborn represents the inheritance or future of Israel. It is the blood on the wooden doorpost that protects this inheritance. This is a foreshadowing of the final sacrifice of the Christ on the cross. Hear the firstborn will be sacrificed for the final salvation of not only Israel but all mankind. Let us summarize the symbolism of The Passover. First we have the lamb, which will represent the Lamb of God (the Christ). Next we will see that the whole lamb is sacrificed, which represents the complete sacrifice of the Christ. The blood of the sacrifice will be spilt on the wood of the doorpost, and with the Christ on the wooden cross. This spilt blood will protect the inheritance of Israel at the Passover, and on the cross will not only protect, but allow for the complete and final redemption of sin. The dinner with the bitter herbs and unleavened bread will symbolize the pain and suffering of the cross. The eating of the meal standing and fully dressed will represent the journey from sin to salvation as we partake of this sacrifice. The sacrifice of the Passover becomes the cross of the church. The Passover saves the first born of Israel and the cross saves all mankind.

THE LAW

As Israel leaves Egypt, it also leaves behind its laws, gods and government. Israel is not yet a nation. Israel is a mob of people, over 2 (two) million strong, without a government or a set of laws. There is nothing to hold the people together. Moses takes the people to Mt. Sinai where God establishes the nation of Israel.

You might ask, what does this have to do with sacrifice, and the answer of course is everything. Israel is to be established as a nation of the "Living God". It must have a set of rules and laws that not only allow for the orderly administration of the running of the government, but also establish the rule of God. All of this will be accomplished at Mt. Sinai.

It is at Mt. Sinai that the Bible, for the first time, defines exactly what sin is in terms of human interactions. We see first that there are four commandments dealing with our interaction with God, and then six commandments dealing with our interactions with mankind. With these Ten Commandments God defines the limits of our acceptable conduct if we are to be able to interact with Him. We see the whole range of both acceptable and unacceptable actions spelled out for mankind. It would be unfair to state that God had not told mankind of these rules before Mt. Sinai. Rather, this is where they are recorded for all history. It is hear where we can look back and see the conduct that God expects from each of us.

This conduct is first described as our relationship to God. God is to be first in our lives, we are to have no other gods or make graven images to worship, we are to refrain from using God's name in vain, and we are to keep the Sabbath as a holy day.

After we make our commitment to God, we to address our relationship to the rest of mankind. We are to honor our parents, not kill, not commit adultery, not steal, not lie about our neighbors, and not covet what our neighbors possess.

These Ten Commandments were later restated by the Christ in to two short commandments. We are to honor God above all else and love our neighbors in the same way we love ourselves. It should be noted that the Christ's restating of the Ten Commandments was not meant to remove them, but to help us understand them by explaining them in a different way.

Now that sin is defined, we can grade ourselves by how we obey these commandments. Even a causal observation will show that we break these commandments on a regular basis. That being true, we can now look to what is the punishment for braking them, and how we can fulfil that punishment so that we might be restored in our fellowship with God. Now we can see the purpose of sacrifice. God ordained sacrifice to Adam and Eve when He killed the animal to make their clothing. Sacrifice is to be the payment for sin. The blood of the sacrifice is to be used to cover up the sin until the price is paid. In Abraham's life we see that the animal sacrifice is to be replaced with a human sacrifice. We also find those famous words of Abraham *"My son, God will provide himself a lamb for a burnt offering:"* Here we are told that the sacrifice will be provided by God, and not by us. If this is indeed the case, how and when will God provide the sacrifice? Now we can turn to the plan God has provided and see how the payment for sin is made. Let us look at the Kinsman Redeemer.

CHAPTER 4
THE LAW OF THE KINSMAN REDEEMER

The concept of the Kinsman Redeemer was evident even at the time of Adam and Eve. Eve believed that Cain was to be that redeemer. In Genesis 4:1 we find:

> *"And Adam knew Eve his wife; and she conceived, and bare Cain, and said, I have gotten a man from the LORD."*

It was Eve's belief that Cain would be the Kinsman Redeemer, who would restore her family to God's fold. Even at the beginning of time, we see the promise made and the hope for the Redeemer. For Eve, it was not to be, but she taught the lessons to her sons, and they in turn passed it on in turn to their families.

We next see this concept in the story of Job. Having lost everything and being chastised by his friends, Job makes an incredible statement of faith. In Job 19:25 we find these words:

> *"For I know that my redeemer liveth, And that he shall stand at the latter day upon the earth:"*

The Hebrew word translated as redeemer is more properly translated as Kinsman Redeemer. In the Hebrew it implies one who meets the requirements of a kinsman redeemer.

To better understand this concept of the kinsman redeemer we must look to the laws Moses brought back to the people of Israel from Mount Sinai. This is recorded in Leviticus 25:23-55:

> *"The land shall not be sold for ever: for the land is mine; for ye are strangers and sojourners with me. And in all the land of your possession ye shall grant a redemption for the land. If thy brother be waxen poor, and hath sold away some of his possession, and if any of his kin come to redeem it, then shall he redeem that which his brother sold. And if the man have none to redeem it, and himself be able to redeem it; Then let him count the years of the sale*

thereof, and restore the overplus unto the man to whom he sold it; that he may return unto his possession. But if he be not able to restore it to him, then that which is sold shall remain in the hand of him that hath bought it until the year of jubile: and in the jubile it shall go out, and he shall return unto his possession. And if a man sell a dwelling house in a walled city, then he may redeem it within a whole year after it is sold; within a full year may he redeem it. And if it be not redeemed within the space of a full year, then the house that is in the walled city shall be established for ever to him that bought it throughout his generations: it shall not go out in the jubile. But the houses of the villages which have no wall round about them shall be counted as the fields of the country: they may be redeemed, and they shall go out in the jubile. Notwithstanding the cities of the Levites, and the houses of the cities of their possession, may the Levites redeem at any time. And if a man purchase of the Levites, then the house that was sold, and the city of his possession, shall go out in the year of jubile: for the houses of the cities of the Levites are their possession among the children of Israel. But the field of the suburbs of their cities may not be sold; for it is their perpetual possession.

And if thy brother be waxen poor, and fallen in decay with thee; then thou shalt relieve him: yea, though he be a stranger, or a sojourner; that he may live with thee. Take thou no usury of him, or increase: but fear thy God; that thy brother may live with thee. Thou shalt not give him thy money upon usury, nor lend him thy victuals for increase. I am the L ORD *your God, which brought you forth out of the land of Egypt, to give you the land of Canaan, and to be your God.*

And if thy brother that dwelleth by thee be waxen poor, and be sold unto thee; thou shalt not compel him to serve as a bondservant: But as an hired servant, and as a sojourner, he shall be with thee, and shall serve thee unto the year of jubile: And then shall he depart from thee, both he and his children with him, and shall return unto his own family, and unto the possession of his fathers shall he return. For they are my servants, which I brought forth out of the land of Egypt: they shall not be sold as bondmen. Thou shalt not rule over him with rigour; but shalt fear thy God. Both thy bondmen, and thy bondmaids, which thou shalt have, shall be of the heathen that are round about you; of them shall ye buy bondmen and bondmaids. Moreover of the children of the strangers that do sojourn among you, of them shall ye buy, and of their families that are with you, which they begat in your land: and they shall be your possession. And ye shall take them as an inheritance for your children after you, to inherit them for a possession; they shall be your bondmen for ever: but over your brethren the children of Israel, ye shall not rule one over another with rigour.

And if a sojourner or stranger wax rich by thee, and thy brother that dwelleth by him wax poor, and sell himself unto the stranger or sojourner by thee, or to the stock of the stranger's family: After that he is sold he may be redeemed again; one of his brethren may redeem him: Either his uncle, or his uncle's son, may redeem him, or any that is nigh of kin unto him of his family may redeem him; or if he be able, he may redeem himself. And he shall reckon with him that bought him from the year that he was sold to him unto the year of jubile: and the price of his sale shall be according unto the number of years, according to the time of an hired servant shall it be with him. If there be yet many years behind, according unto them he shall give again the price of his redemption out of the money that he was bought for. And if there remain but few years unto the year of jubile, then he shall count with him, and according unto his years shall he give him again the price of his redemption. And as a yearly hired servant shall he be with him: and the other shall not rule with rigour over him in thy sight. And if he be not redeemed in these years, then he shall go out in the year of jubile, both he, and his children with him. For unto me the children of Israel are servants; they are my servants whom I brought forth out of the land of Egypt: I am the LORD your God."

At this point we need to stop and see if we can understand the underlying principals set forth by this passage. To set the stage, Israel is at Mount Sinai having just left Egypt. They are not a nation, but a mob of people, having no government, no laws, no culture, no religion, and without a leader. The purpose of the stop at Mount Sinai is to establish these things. Moses goes up on the mountain for 40 days and God delivers all of these to the people. Without going through all of the steps here, at the end of the process, Israel is now a nation with all the requirements of being a nation met.

The passage above describes the use of and the dividing of the land Israel has been promised. The first point to note, is that the land was to be divided among the tribes, and the tribes would divide it among their members. Every member of every tribe was to have their own land. The second point was that none of the land was to be owned, but was held in trust for God, with each family being responsible to God for their portion. Since no one owned the land, the land could not be bought or sold. If a family was unable to care for themselves or the land, they could mortgage their portion to another Jew, and receive benefits from the mortgage. The person loaning the money would have the use of the land until either one of two events happened. Either the land was redeemed by the original family, or at the year of the jubilee the land would be returned free and clear to the original family.

In another section of Leviticus, we see God's instruction for the care of the land. The land was to be worked for six years, and on the seventh year the land was to lie fallow. Then the land was worked for another six years. This was to continue for seven cycles of seven years. After the forty-ninth year the land was to lie fallow for an additional year, called the year of the jubilee. On this special year, all debts between Jews were cancelled and all land was returned to the original family before a new cycle was started. This way, both the land and the family were preserved. Isn't it wonderful that God created a plan that took care of both the land and the people?

Notice, that even if the family was unable to redeem the land, it would automatically happen in the year of the jubilee. However, there is a provision in the law, which allows a family to redeem the land before the year of the jubilee. If a family has the means to repay the loan earlier, the land must be returned to them when they ask for it. This was to protect the inheritance of the family.

As most of us know, it is hard to get out of debt, and to repay mortgages. There was also included a second provision in the law that allowed a close relative (Kinsman Redeemer) to buy back the mortgage for the family. This also required that the land be returned when the debt is settled. There are four specific requirements for the Kinsman Redeemer to meet in order for this to take place.

1. The first requirement is that the Kinsman Redeemer be a close relative. The closer the better.
2. The second requirement is that the relative must be asked by the one needing to be redeemed. The Kinsman Redeemer could not act on his own without being asked by the one needing to be redeemed. It was also required that the Kinsman Redeemer be the closest member to the family. If there was a closer kin, they must be asked first. There was a strict order in which they must be asked.
3. The third requirement was that they must be able to redeem the mortgage. If the one asked did not have the means to redeem the debt, they were excused from the responsibility, and the family could ask another relative who was not as close. It was viewed as the family's responsibility to take care of the family first.
4. The fourth requirement was that the Kinsman Redeemer be willing to redeem the family. While there were many forces acting to make the Kinsman Redeemer redeem the debt, it ultimately was their decision and they could choose not to redeem the debt.

As we can easily see from this, both the land and the family were given protection in God's plan for the Promised Land. No family could ever lose the legacy of the land. This was also extended to the family. If a brother was to die without children, it was the responsibility of his brother to take the wife into his family as another wife, and their first son was to be declared the son of his brother, who then would inherit the land and keep his brother's name alive in Israel. The protections of the Kinsman Redeemer were both for the land and the family.

The book of Ruth is a good example of how this would work, and is a book everyone who is interested in the concept of the Kinsman Redeemer should read. We will not go through it line by line in this discussion, but I will try to summarize it for the reader.

The story begins as Naomi, her husband and two children leave the Promised Land for Moab, due to a drought in Israel. While living in

Moab, both of Naomi's sons marry women of Moab. Naomi's husband dies, and then both of her children die without having children themselves. This leaves the family without anyone to redeem the land back in Israel. Naomi vows to return to Israel and frees her daughter-in-laws to return to their families. Ruth makes the decision to return to Israel with Naomi and continue to take care of her. We must remember that Ruth has no standing in Israel since she is not a Jew. In spite of this they return to Israel, and Naomi instructs Ruth in the social welfare plan God has set up in Israel for people who are unable to take care of themselves. Part of the law required that when the harvest was gathered, some of the crop was to be left in the fields, and those without a means of taking care of themselves were allowed to harvest the leftovers as a way of surviving. Notice, that unlike our system today, God's plan provides for those who are willing to go get help. If you stayed at home in Israel, you could die of starvation, but if you went to the fields, there was food you could collect to stay alive. Naomi tells Ruth whose field to harvest. Boaz was a close relation to Naomi's husband. Ruth without knowing how all of this works does as Naomi requests and works in Boaz's fields. At the proper time, Naomi tells Ruth to inform Boaz who she was married to, and to request him to be her Kinsman Redeemer. Boaz being aware of her situation and his own responsibilities, begins the process to help her. Notice, that first of all Boaz is a close relative, and that Ruth has requested help. This meets two of the four requirements of the Kinsman Redeemer. We can also see that Boaz meets the last two requirements, in that he is rich (we know that from the fact Ruth is working in his fields) and that he is willing.

There is now a problem that must be addressed, in that Boaz is NOT the closest relative to Ruth. Boaz cannot be the Kinsman Redeemer as long as there is someone closer in relation to Ruth who is willing to become the Kinsman Redeemer. Boaz goes to see this relative and discusses the situation with him. This relative meets the first three conditions of the Kinsman Redeemer, but is unwilling to become the Kinsman Redeemer due to his family situation. This leaves Boaz free to fulfil the role of the Kinsman Redeemer. He marries Ruth, and the result of the marriage is that David is their grandson. Ruth goes from being nothing to the grandmother of David by following God's plan that was laid out 1,500 years before at Mount Sinai.

This lays out the law and the culture that was Israel, but what does it have to do with our discussion of Salvation and the Christ. In the next chapter we will look at the true Kinsman Redeemer.

CHAPTER 5
THE TRUE KINSMAN REDEEMER

We have had a remarkable journey as we have looked at first the concept of sacrifice and the need for the sacrifice, then through the law of the Kinsman Redeemer in Jewish law to finally finish here with the true Kinsman Redeemer. I am sure some of you are thinking what does all of this have to do with God and salvation.

Let us start this final section with the question, why does God even care about our salvation. As we began our discussion, we find that we were created for the purpose of being able to choose to commune with our creator. He determined that it must be a free will choice on our part to commune with Him, and that we could not be forced or coerced into that choice. The problem with this is that we chose to sin which puts us into conflict with the creator.

Since the creator of the universe created it with rules, He followed these rules. Sin must be paid for with a sacrifice, and as we learned earlier, the sacrifice must be perfect and be a close relation to the sinner.

Three events in the Old Testament tie all of this together. First, an animal had to die in order to illustrate the need for sacrifice to Adam and Eve. The animal paid the price for their sin, and was used to cover their nakedness before God. Secondly, Abram was told by God to sacrifice his first born son. God did not do this with the intention to actually kill Isaac, but to illustrate how the final sacrifice must be made. An innocent relation of the sinner must pay the price. The final clue is in the law of the Kinsman Redeemer. It shows us that a close member of the family of the sinner will be allowed to redeem the sinner.

THE OLD TESTAMENT SPEAKS

There are several passages in the Old Testament that speak to this issue. The first on is found in Numbers 5:5–8:

> *And the* LORD *spake unto Moses, saying, Speak unto the children of Israel, When a man or woman shall commit any*

> *sin that men commit, to do a trespass against the LORD, and that person be guilty; Then they shall confess their sin which they have done: and he shall recompense his trespass with the principal thereof, and add unto it the fifth part thereof, and give it unto him against whom he hath trespassed. But if the man have no kinsman to recompense the trespass unto, let the trespass be recompensed unto the LORD, even to the priest; beside the ram of the atonement, whereby an atonement shall be made for him.*

We can see that the law specifically speaks to trespass (sin) being redeemed by a relative, and if there is no relative capable of the redemption, than it is to be brought to God for redemption.

In Exodus 6:6–7, we can see that God informs Israel that He would be the one who would bring them out of bondage (sin). It is God as the redeemer who rescues Israel:

> *Wherefore say unto the children of Israel, I am the LORD, and I will bring you out from under the burdens of the Egyptians, and I will rid you out of their bondage, and I will redeem you with a stretched out arm, and with great judgments: And I will take you to me for a people, and I will be to you a God: and ye shall know that I am the LORD your God, which bringeth you out from under the burdens of the Egyptians*

At the time of David, Samuel reminds Israel that it was necessary for God to redeem them. Samuel is very specific in stating that God is the one to redeem Israel. In 2 Samuel 7:22–24 we find:

> *Wherefore thou art great, O LORD God: for there is none like thee, neither is there any God beside thee, according to all that we have heard with our ears. And what one nation in the earth is like thy people, even like Israel, whom God went to redeem for a people to himself, and to make him a name, and to do for you great things and terrible, for thy land, before thy people, which thou redeemedst to thee from Egypt, from the nations and their gods? For thou hast confirmed to thyself thy people Israel to be a people unto thee for ever: and thou, LORD, art become their God.*

Again, at the time of the captivity Isaiah reminds Israel that it is God who has done the redemption before, and that it will be God who will Redeem Israel again. In prophesy of the last days, Isaiah tells Israel that God will call Israel from the ends of the earth to return to the Promised Land that He has given them. Isaiah 43:1-7 records these words:

But now thus saith the LORD that created thee, O Jacob, And he that formed thee, O Israel, Fear not: for I have redeemed thee, I have called thee by thy name; thou art mine. When thou passest through the waters, I will be with thee; And through the rivers, they shall not overflow thee: When thou walkest through the fire, thou shalt not be burned; Neither shall the flame kindle upon thee. For I am the LORD thy God, The Holy One of Israel, thy Saviour: I gave Egypt for thy ransom, Ethiopia and Seba for thee. Since thou wast precious in my sight, Thou hast been honourable, and I have loved thee: Therefore will I give men for thee, And people for thy life. Fear not: for I am with thee: I will bring thy seed from the east, And gather thee from the west; I will say to the north, Give up; And to the south, Keep not back: Bring my sons from far, And my daughters from the ends of the earth; Even every one that is called by my name: For I have created him for my glory, I have formed him; yea, I have made him.

While this is a prophesy of the end times, it speaks of a redeemed Israel that will return to the Promised Land and be with God.

Again, a little later in the book, Isaiah again refers to God as the redeemer. From this we can see that the accepted role of God was to be the redeemer of Israel. Follow what Isaiah has to say in this passage Isaiah 54:5-8:

For thy Maker is thine husband; The LORD of hosts is his name; And thy Redeemer the Holy One of Israel; The God of the whole earth shall he be called. For the LORD hath called thee as a woman forsaken and grieved in spirit, And a wife of youth, when thou wast refused, saith thy God. For a small moment have I forsaken thee; But with great mercies will I gather thee. In a little wrath I hid my face from thee for a moment; But with everlasting kindness will I have mercy on thee, Saith the LORD thy Redeemer.

Finally, in the book of Jeremiah we can follow this theme of God as the redeemer. Jeremiah reminds Israel that God has redeemed them in the past and will redeem them again. Jeremiah writes in Jeremiah 50:33–34:

> *Thus saith the LORD of hosts; The children of Israel and the children of Judah were oppressed together: And all that took them captives held them fast; They refused to let them go. Their Redeemer is strong; The LORD of hosts is his name: He shall throughly plead their cause, That he may give rest to the land, And disquiet the inhabitants of Babylon.*

This would lead to the Jewish concept of the Messiah (redeemer). The Messiah would be the redeemer of God who would restore Israel to their rightful place with God. Unfortunately as with many great truths, the message is twisted and turned until it comes to mean something entirely different from the original message. By the time of Christ, the message had been changed to state the Messiah would be a man who would come and liberate Israel from its oppressors and return Israel to the glory of David's kingdom. Gone is the message of redemption and returning to God, now the message is one of earthly power. It is easy to see why everyone was so surprised by Christ's message, which was the original message of redeemer who would return mankind to a state of grace with God. Even when Christ tells them He has not come to establish an earthly kingdom, but to establish a heavenly kingdom, no one believes Him.

CHRIST THE KINSMAN REDEEMER

How do we get from sacrifice to the Kinsman Redeemer of Israel to Christ as the Kinsman Redeemer of the world?

First we should look at Bible. The Bible serves as a textbook of God's plan for mankind, and as an instruction book for righteous living. It is progressive in nature, starting with simple concepts and increasing knowledge and understanding as we proceed through the book.

We can follow this logic as we proceed to understand Christ as the Kinsman Redeemer. It starts with God informing Adam and Eve they must pay a price for their sin. God illustrates this by killing the animal and making them clothing. God also teaches them the concept of sacrifice and explains that He will send a redeemer to restore them to righteousness. This process is expanded when Abram is told to sacrifice Isaac and then is instructed that God Himself will provide the sacrifice. At the same time, we find that Job understands this concept and makes the proclamation that he knows that his redeemer lives. Later as Israel leaves Egypt God hands down the Law to Moses, and in the Law we find the human concept of the Kinsman redeemer found in Leviticus. This is further explained in the book of Ruth, as we see the practical example of how it was used by Israel. The result of the book of Ruth, is that a family is redeemed, and the grandson of that family is King David. David understands these concepts as he speaks after his son dies, saying that his son can no longer come to him, but that he is assured that he (David) will be able to go to his son. All through the prophets, we continue to see God revealing the concept of the Kinsman Redeemer who will redeem Israel. It is about this time that the name is changed to the Messiah, who will come to restore Israel. Finally we have the culmination of this with Christ (The Messiah) being born and paying the price of redemption.

Now let us look at Christ as the Kinsman Redeemer, to see if He fulfills the requirements for this office. As you will remember, there are 4 (four) conditions for the Kinsman Redeemer. The Kinsman Redeemer must be a close relative, must have the ability to be the redeemer, must have the willingness to be the redeemer, and finally must be asked to be the redeemer. We will now look at each of these requirements as they relate to Christ.

The first requirement is that he must be a close relative. The term "son of man" is used 43 (forty three) times in the New Testament to refer to Christ. It is the name Christ chooses for himself. Christ is reminding us that even though He is God, He chose to come to earth to become a man, just like all of us. He is choosing to become our relative. Christ is establishing 2 (two) principals by using this name. The first is that he has become man just as we are, and the second is that all mankind is related. We are all sons of Adam, and thus we are all related. This means that Christ is our kinsman.

The second requirement is that the redeemer must be capable of making the payment for the redemption. The Bible records that the payment for sin is the blood sacrifice of perfect man. We are also told, that God Himself will prepare the necessary sacrifice. In Isaiah 53:1-12, we find the very description of the sacrifice and the one who will make it:

> "Who hath believed our report? and to whom is the arm of the LORD revealed For he shall grow up before him as a tender plant, and as a root out of a dry ground: he hath no form nor comeliness; and when we shall see him, there is no beauty that we should desire him. He is despised and rejected of men; a man of sorrows, and

acquainted with grief: and we hid as it were our faces from him; he was despised, and we esteemed him not.

Surely he hath borne our griefs, and carried our sorrows: yet we did esteem him stricken, smitten of God, and afflicted. But he was wounded for our transgressions, he was bruised for our iniquities: the chastisement of our peace was upon him; and with his stripes we are healed. All we like sheep have gone astray; we have turned every one to his own way; and the LORD hath laid on him the iniquity of us all. He was oppressed, and he was afflicted, yet he opened not his mouth: he is brought as a lamb to the slaughter, and as a sheep before her shearers is dumb, so he openeth not his mouth. He was taken from prison and from judgment: and who shall declare his generation? for he was cut off out of the land of the living: for the transgression of my people was he stricken. And he made his grave with the wicked, and with the rich in his death; because he had done no violence, neither was any deceit in his mouth.

Yet it pleased the LORD to bruise him; he hath put him to grief: when thou shalt make his soul an offering for sin, he shall see his seed, he shall prolong his days, and the pleasure of the LORD shall prosper in his hand. He shall see of the travail of his soul, and shall be satisfied: by his knowledge shall my righteous servant justify many; for he shall bear their iniquities. Therefore will I divide him a portion with the great, and he shall divide the spoil with the strong; because he hath poured out his soul unto death: and he was numbered with the transgressors; and he bare the sin of many, and made intercession for the transgressors."

This passage describes one who has come from God, who is perfect and has no sin, but who is condemned and dies for the sins of people. This is Isaiah's description of the Messiah (Kinsman Redeemer) who will redeem Israel (mankind). We can easily see that God has sent Christ as the sacrifice for the sins of the world, and that He meets the requirement of the Kinsman Redeemer. We must also look to one other requirement in this section. As we saw earlier in the book of Ruth, even though Boaz was a kinsman of Ruth, he was not the closest. Is there another who stands closer in line as our kinsman? Christ is the only one found capable of making the payment. In the book of Revelation 5:1-12 we find the following passage relating how Christ has become the Kinsman Redeemer:

> "And I saw in the right hand of him that sat on the throne a book written within and on the backside, sealed with seven seals. And I saw a strong angel proclaiming with a loud voice, Who is worthy to open the book, and to loose the seals thereof? And no man in heaven, nor in earth, neither under the earth, was able to open the book, neither to look thereon. And I wept much, because no man was found worthy to open and to read the book, neither to look thereon. And one of the elders saith unto me, Weep not: behold, the Lion of the tribe of Juda, the Root of David, hath prevailed to open the book, and to loose the seven seals thereof.
>
> And I beheld, and, lo, in the midst of the throne and of the four beasts, and in the midst of the elders, stood a Lamb as it had been slain, having seven horns and seven eyes, which are the seven Spirits of God sent forth into all the earth. And he came and took the book out of the right hand of him that sat upon the throne. And when he had taken the book, the four beasts and four and twenty elders fell down before the Lamb, having every one of them harps, and golden vials full of odours, which are the prayers of saints. And they sung a new song, saying, Thou art worthy to take the book, and to open the seals thereof: for thou wast slain, and hast redeemed us to God by thy blood out of every kindred, and tongue, and people, and nation; And hast made us unto our God kings and priests: and we shall reign on the earth. And I beheld, and I heard the voice of many angels round about the throne and the beasts and the elders: and the number of them was ten thousand times ten thousand, and thousands of thousands; Saying with a loud voice, Worthy is the Lamb that was slain to receive power, and riches, and wisdom, and strength, and honour, and glory, and blessing.

We see that at first no one is found with the ability to pay the price, and as John weeps, Christ appears and is found worthy to redeem. The book discussed here is the title deed to the earth. It was originally held by Adam, who mortgaged it to Satan with his sin. Notice that God still holds the deed, and what Christ is redeeming is the mortgage to all the earth. His blood sacrifice has paid the price of redemption. We also see, that the price has been paid with a blood sacrifice. This also assures us that Christ was willing to pay the price. In Matthew 26:36–46 we find Christ the night before He died praying to God, first that God will not require Him to die for the salvation of mankind, but then Christ concludes His prayer by stating that it is God's will that will be done, not Christ's.

> "Then cometh Jesus with them unto a place called Gethsemane, and saith unto the disciples, Sit ye here, while I go and pray yonder. And he took with him Peter and the two sons of Zebedee, and began to be sorrowful and very heavy. Then saith he unto them, My soul is exceeding sorrowful, even unto death: tarry ye here, and watch with me. And he went a little further, and fell on his face, and prayed, saying, O my Father, if it be possible, let this cup pass from me: nevertheless not as I will, but as thou wilt. And he cometh unto the disciples, and findeth them asleep, and saith unto Peter, What, could ye not watch with me one hour? Watch and pray, that ye enter not into temptation: the spirit indeed is willing, but the flesh is weak. He went away again the second time, and prayed, saying, O my Father, if this cup may not pass away from me, except I drink it, thy will be done. And he came and found them asleep again: for their eyes were heavy. And he left them, and went away again, and prayed the third time, saying the same words. Then cometh he to his disciples, and saith unto them, Sleep on now, and take your rest: behold, the hour is at hand, and the Son of man is betrayed into the hands of sinners. Rise, let us be going: behold, he is at hand that doth betray me."

The next day at about 3:00 P.M. in the afternoon as the Christ hung on the cross He pays the price and accepts our sins. We know this from the words written in both Matthew and Mark's Gospels (Mark 15:34):

> *"And at the ninth hour Jesus cried with a loud voice, saying, Eloi, Eloi, lama sabachthani? which is, being interpreted, My God, my God, why hast thou forsaken me?"*

As the Christ accepts our sins, the Creator must turn His back on His only son. God cannot allow sin to come into His presence and thus He turns His back on the Christ. For the first time since the creation God and Christ are separated. Since God cannot allow sin in His presence, Christ must bear the burden alone. This death alone, without God is the price Christ paid for our sins. This is what Christ was concerned about the night before when He prayed to God to see if there was another way. There was no other way and we see Christ pays the price.

This is a very sad time for all Christians, as we see Christ suffering on the cross in payment for our debt. Also to know that He is doing this without the help of the Creator. Will He be able to complete the task given Him by the Father? If we look to John's gospel (John 19:30) we find these words:

> *"When Jesus therefore had received the vinegar, he said, It is finished: and he bowed his head, and gave up the ghost."*

Look at these words. Christ does NOT say that He is finished, He says "IT" is finished. He is not ending His life with a whimper of defeat, but with a triumphant shout of victory. The "IT" He is talking about is redemption for all of mankind. He has paid the price of the Kinsman Redeemer, and can now return mankind to their rightful place in communion with the Father. This is the last act needed to complete the requirements of the Kinsman Redeemer.

As we have seen, Christ by His own choice has become our Kinsman Redeemer, has lived a life that gives him the ability to be our Kinsman Redeemer, and has of His own choice, chosen to become our Kinsman Redeemer. All of the requirements of salvation (redemption) have been met. We can now truly become the sons and daughters of the Creator.

One element is still missing. God's work is done. There only remains the last requirement of the Kinsman Redeemer. Remember Boaz could not become the kinsman redeemer of Ruth until she asked for his help. God also cannot become our kinsman redeemer until we ask. In the final chapter we will discuss this final action of redemption.

CHAPTER 6
YOUR CHOICE

Two thousand years ago the fate of the world was settled. God completed the requirements of the Kinsman Redeemer. The plan outlined in the book of Leviticus was completed and salvation (redemption) was completed for the entire world. The three requirements God needed to complete were done, and the only remaining requirement was for us to ask the Kinsman Redeemer to help us.

If you have reached this position in the book without having asked the Kinsman Redeemer for help, it is now your turn to make a choice. Unique among all of God's creation, man is the only creature with the ability to make a conscious decision. At this point you must ask the Kinsman Redeemer for His help. You may be conflicted as to whether you should ask for help, or how you can ask for help. In this chapter we will look at the facts you will need to make the correct decision.

Paul in writing to the church in Rome attempts to answer the questions we ask concerning the Kinsman Redeemer, and our need for assistance. We will look at what is commonly called the *"Romans Road"*. The *"Romans Road"* is a series of passages in the book of Romans that lead us to a decision concerning the Kinsman Redeemer.

The first question that must be answered is "Do I need help?" If you are content with your life and do not care about those things that separate you from God, then the answer is NO. If you realize that there should be more to life, or you are not content with how the world is living then, the answer is probably. Think for a minute. What can you do to change either the world or even your own life? The answer is of course that there is nothing we can do. Many of us try to change ourselves for the better, but our old nature comes right back. In Romans 7:14–25 Paul describes how we lead our lives. We try to do right, but will always fail and do just the exact opposite of what we should do.

> *"For we know that the Law is spiritual, but I am of flesh, sold into bondage to sin. For what I am doing, I do not understand; for I am not practicing what I would like to do, but I am doing the very thing I hate. But if I do the very thing I do not want to do, I agree with the Law, confessing*

that the Law is good. So now, no longer am I the one doing it, but sin which dwells in me. For I know that nothing good dwells in me, that is, in my flesh; for the willing is present in me, but the doing of the good is not. For the good that I want, I do not do, but I practice the very evil that I do not want. But if I am doing the very thing I do not want, I am no longer the one doing it, but sin which dwells in me. I find then the principle that evil is present in me, the one who wants to do good. For I joyfully concur with the law of God in the inner man, but I see a different law in the members of my body, waging war against the law of my mind and making me a prisoner of the law of sin which is in my members. Wretched man that I am! Who will set me free from the body of this death? Thanks be to God through Jesus Christ our Lord! So then, on the one hand I myself with my mind am serving the law of God, but on the other, with my flesh the law of sin."

We have all made at least one decision to disobey. We have used our free will to decide to do it our way instead of God's way. Paul describes it this way in Romans 3:23.

"For all have sinned, and come short of the glory of God"

We can also see that there is a price for living our lives the way we do. As children we learned that there was a punishment for disobeying our parents. When we disobeyed (sinned) they were forced to punish us. Later in life we have seen the price that our friends and family have made for disobeying the rules of society. Divorce, drugs, alcohol, and sexual pervasion have led to much suffering and punishment.

In Romans 6:23, Paul again summarizes this concept of punishment for our failings (sin):

"For the wages of sin is death; but the gift of God is eternal life through Jesus Christ our Lord."

The price of our sin is death. The only choice is who will pay the price. We can refuse the help of the Kinsman Redeemer and pay the price of death and eternal separation from the Creator ourselves, or we can ask for the help of the Kinsman Redeemer, who has already paid the price for us.

Again, Paul writing to the church in Rome explains that Christ has already paid the price as the Kinsman Redeemer. In Romans 5:8–9 we see:

> *"But God commendeth his love toward us, in that, while we were yet sinners, Christ died for us. Much more then, being now justified by his blood, we shall be saved from wrath through him."*

We can see here that God through Christ has paid the price of the Kinsman Redeemer for all sin for all time. We can receive the redemption offered by Christ as our Kinsman Redeemer by following the outline set forth in Leviticus. All of the steps necessary to conform to the rule of the Kinsman Redeemer have been met except the last one illustrated in the book of Ruth. We must ask if we are to be redeemed.

In his letter to the church at Roman, Paul summarizes this last step in the process of receiving the rewards promised in the law of the Kinsman Redeemer. In Romans 10:9-13 we find this statement:

> *"The word is nigh thee, even in thy mouth, and in thy heart: that is, the word of faith, which we preach; That if thou shalt confess with thy mouth the Lord Jesus, and shalt believe in thine heart that God hath raised him from the dead, thou shalt be saved. For with the heart man believeth unto righteousness; and with the mouth confession is made unto salvation. For the scripture saith, Whosoever believeth on him shall not be ashamed. For there is no difference between the Jew and the Greek: for the same Lord over all is rich unto all that call upon him. For whosoever shall call upon the name of the Lord shall be saved."*

The whosoever here is YOU. The final step in God's plan of redemption is for you to ask. Everything else is done, all that remains is for you to ask. It is NOT possible to redeem yourself, it can only be done through God's plan, and your only responsibility is to ask

You may now be thinking of the last question you ever need to have answered about God's plan. The question is how do I ask? Many people would tell you that you need to pray to God and ask for His forgiveness. It is possible that you have never prayed and do not know how. Let's look at a solution together.

As we have seen, God, has chosen to be our close relative. That is what makes the whole concept work. How would you talk to your parents or closest friend and ask for their help? That is what you must do now. Talk to God as you would your closest friend. This is not a matter of religion or dogma. This is a matter of two friends ending the conflict between them and restoring their relationship to that of best friends again.

The basics of the conversation should be as follows:

I am a mess, and have been unable to do what is right and what I should do in my life.

I have tried to change and have been unable to do it by myself

I need someone to help me change and become the person I should be.

God I ask you to help me. Forgive the things I have done wrong, and make me the person I should be. I am asking for the help of the Kinsman Redeemer to pay the price that I cannot pay and make me whole again.

Thank you God for paying the price and allowing me to come home.

Amen

This is sometimes called the *"Sinners Prayer"*, and the words themselves are not important. The statements above will NOT save you. It is not necessary to repeat them as written. They are merely a guide you can use in your conversation with God. It is the meaning behind the words that makes it all work. If you are truly sorry for your sins and ask for forgiveness, God will forgive you and restore you to a state of righteousness.

THE NEXT STEP

Once you have asked for God's help and accepted the free gift of the Kinsman Redeemer, you are ready to move on to service in God's kingdom.

May I suggest the following steps?

- Find a *"Bible Believing"* church and talk to the pastor about your decision.
- Leave behind those friends and situations that caused the problem in your life and look to fellow Christians for friendship and help.
- Center your life on the church and the work of the church, so that you have something to replace the things that caused your problem.
- Study God's word (The Bible) and learn the lessons God has prepared for you.
- Share the good news of your redemption with others.

This last step is most important in confirming your decision to change. The last message Christ left for Christians is found in Acts 1:8. It is a simple message that we must continue to share the message of the Kinsman Redeemer with all who need it.

> *"But ye shall receive power, after that the Holy Ghost is come upon you: and ye shall be witnesses unto me both in Jerusalem, and in all Judaea, and in Samaria, and unto the uttermost part of the earth."*

This does not require that you become a *"Holy Joe"* or a fanatic, but that you simply share what Christ has done for you. Explain how you have been changed and explain this wonderful concept of the Kinsman Redeemer to those who are in need.

It is my prayer that God will richly bless you and use you in his service.

Made in the USA
Lexington, KY
14 September 2018